What Would You Do?

THE LOUISIANA PURCHASE

Would You Close the Deal?

Elaine Landau

Enslow Elementary
an imprint of

Enslow Publishers, Inc.
40 Industrial Road
Box 398
Berkeley Heights, NJ 07922
USA
http://www.enslow.com

Enslow Elementary, an imprint of Enslow Publishers, Inc.

Enslow Elementary® is a registered trademark of Enslow Publishers, Inc.

Library of Congress Cataloging-in-Publication Data

Landau, Elaine.
  The Louisiana Purchase : would you close the deal? / Elaine Landau.
    p. cm. — (What would you do?)
  Summary: "A basic discussion about the history of the Louisiana Purchase, and how the United States
    expanded their lands by buying the Louisiana Territory from France"—Provided by publisher.
  Includes bibliographical references and index.
  Library Edition ISBN: 978-0-7660-2902-6
  Paperback Edition ISBN: 978-1-59845-196-2
  1. Louisiana Purchase—Juvenile literature. 2. United States—Territorial expansion—Juvenile literature.
    3. Napoleon I, Emperor of the French, 1769–1821—Relations with Americans—Juvenile literature. 4.
    Jefferson, Thomas, 1743–1826—Juvenile literature. I. Title.
  E333.L17 2008
  973.4'6—dc22   2007023372

Printed in the United States of America
012014 Bang Printing, Brainerd, Minn.
10 9 8 7

To Our Readers: We have done our best to make sure all Internet Addresses in this book were active and appropriate when we went to press. However, the author and the publisher have no control over and assume no liability for the material available on those Internet sites or on other Web sites they may link to. Any comments or suggestions can be sent by e-mail to comments@enslow.com or to the address on the back cover.

Every effort has been made to locate all copyright holders of material used in this book. If any errors or omissions have occurred, corrections will be made in future editions of this book.

♻ Enslow Publishers, Inc., is committed to printing our books on recycled paper. The paper in every book contains 10% to 30% post-consumer waste (PCW). The cover board on the outside of each book contains 100% PCW. Our goal is to do our part to help young people and the environment too!

Illustration Credits: ©Corel Corporation, pp. 7, 17, 22;©Enslow Publishers, Inc., pp. 4, 44; ©Jupiter Images, p. 15; Architect of the Capitol, p. 11; Battle on Santo Domingo, a painting by January Suchodolski/Public - domain image from Wikipedia.com, p. 37; CDC (Centers for Disease Control)/ James Gathany, p. 38 (bottom); Clipart.com/© Getty Images, pp. 1, 5, 20, 27, 28, 33, 36, 42; Fotoluminate LLC, Shutterstock, p. 23; iStockphoto/© Getty Images, p. 34; July Flowers/ Shutterstock, p. 9; Kathryn Bell/ Shutterstock, p. 16(top); Louisiana State Museum, p. 18; María Luisa de Parma, 1800, Francisco de Goya y Lucientes/Public -domain image from Wikipedia.com, p. 16; National Archives and Records Administration(NARA), p. 43(right); Photos.com/© Getty Images, pp. 19(top); Public -domain image from Wikipedia.com, pp. 6, 26; Reproduced from *Uniforms of the United States Army*, published by Dover Publications Inc., in 1998, p. 31; The Library of Congress, pp. 33, 40; The Library of Congress, Rare Books and Special Collections Division, p. 29; U.S. Department of the Interior, p. 41(top, right)

Cover Illustration: White House Historical Association

CONTENTS

THE UNITED STATES IN 1800

BRITISH NORTH AMERICA

Great Lakes

CONTINENTAL DIVIDE

Rocky Mountains

MISSISSIPPI RIVER

LOUISIANA TERRITORY

NEW SPAIN

INDIANA TERRITORY

OHIO

PENNSYLVANIA

NEW YORK

MAINE PART OF MA

VT

NH

MA

CT

RI

NJ

MD

DE

VIRGINIA

KENTUCKY

TENNESSEE

NORTH CAROLINA

SOUTH CAROLINA

GEORGIA

MISSISSIPPI TERRITORY

SPANISH FLORIDA

ATLANTIC OCEAN

Gulf of Mexico

States and territories of the United States

Before the Louisiana Purchase, the United States only included most of the land east of the Mississippi River.

A Nation Waiting to Grow

Today the United States is very large. Yet this was not always so.

In 1800, the nation was less than half the size it is today. It only reached as far west as the Mississippi River.

Many Americans dreamed of having a bigger nation. They believed in their way of life. They felt that the United States could be an even greater nation.

These Americans wanted to see their country grow. They hoped that one day the United States would reach

VUE DE LA NOUVELLE ORLÉANS EN 1719

New Orleans was a small town at the mouth of the Mississippi River in 1718.

« Les Iles ou quartiers des Bourgeois sont entourés d'eau pendant trois mois de l'année vu le débordement des eaux du fleuve depuis le 15 mars jusqu'au 24 juin. Devant la ville il y a une levée et par derrière un fossé et autres découlements. »

from the Atlantic to the Pacific coast. Getting more land was not easy, however.

Spain held the land to the west. It was known as the Louisiana **Territory**. The area stretched from the Gulf of Mexico to Canada.

This land once belonged to France. Then in 1762, King Louis XV gave it to his cousin King Charles III of Spain. It was a thank-you gift from France. Spain had helped France in a war against Great Britain.

In 1762, King Louis XV of France gave the Louisiana Territory to King Charles III of Spain (above).

Because of this gift, the United States could not grow bigger. Americans could only settle just past the Appalachian Mountains. There, they cleared the land and grew crops. Trappers and hunters did well in the rich forests.

Yet these **pioneers** needed a way to get their goods to market. There was no direct land route to the East. The mountains made it hard to get there.

So the settlers used the rivers. They put their goods on **flatboats**.

Flatboats were used to travel up and down the Mississippi River. This painting by George Caleb Bingham is called *Jolly Flatboatmen*.

These were floated down the Mississippi River. Some settlers used the Ohio River too.

The goods reached the **port** of New Orleans. From there, they were shipped to ports in the East. Lumber and furs were sent to Europe as well.

Spain owned the port of New Orleans. But American settlers still used it. They also stored their goods there before loading them onto ships.

Americans did not pay to use the port. They could use it for free. This right was promised in a 1795 **treaty**, an agreement that both the Spaniards and Americans signed. It was known as the Treaty of San Lorenzo, or Pinckney's Treaty.

The Mississippi River is the largest river in the United States. During the 1700s and early 1800s it was an important river. Since there were no cars, planes, or trains then, people shipped goods on the river using boats.

Yet as time passed, feelings changed. Many Americans had poured into the area. These settlers used the port quite a lot.

The Spaniards were uneasy about this. They thought there were too many Americans. They did not want them taking over.

WHAT WOULD YOU DO?

What if you were an American in 1800? You are thinking about going west. Many settlers have done quite well there.

Yet you are not sure about going. Would it really be the right move? A lot depends on the treaty with Spain.

You know that treaties have sometimes been broken. Spain could tax Americans to use the port. They could even close it off to them. Then you would be sorry you came.

On the other hand, there might be no problems with the port. You might make a good living in the West. Your family might be happy there too.

Would you . . .

✳ **Take a chance and head west?**

✳ **Be ready to pack your things and go?**

SETTLERS MOVE WEST

Many settlers took a chance and went west to the area between the Appalachian Mountains and the Mississippi River. They came hoping to build a better life for themselves and their families. Some opened new businesses there. Others started large farms. More families kept coming each year. However, things did not always go well for them.

Spain broke the treaty in 1798. Sometimes it closed the New Orleans port to Americans. Other times, Americans had to pay a tax to use it.

The American settlers grew very angry. They felt that Spain was being unfair. The settlers feared that they would not be able to make a living. They wanted help from their government. Yet little was done for them.

The government was in the East. The settlers were way out west. There was no railroad connecting the East and the

West back then. At times, it took weeks or even months to get a letter from another part of the country. Sometimes, the settlers felt forgotten. This only added to their anger.

These people are on their way west.

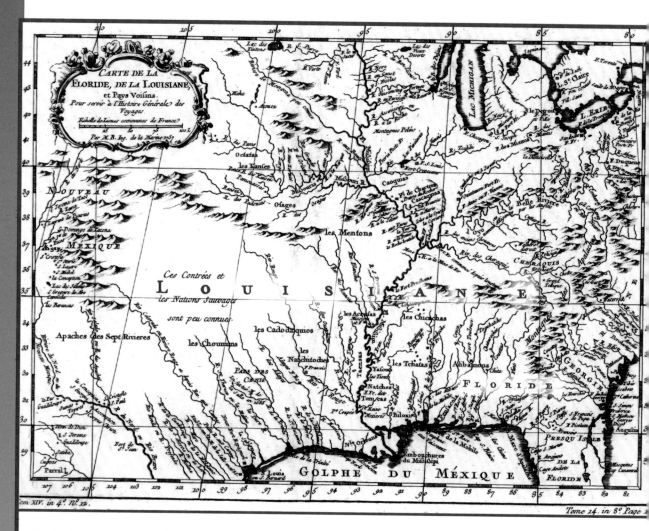

This French map from 1757 shows how people thought the Florida and Louisiana territories looked. The French used the spellings "Louisiane" and "Floride."

WHAT WOULD YOU DO?

What if you were a fur trader? Your business is in the West. Now you need to get your **pelts**, or animal furs, to ports in the East.

Would you . . .

* Think about moving into Spanish territory? You could become a Spanish citizen. Spain will let anyone who does this use the port for free.

* Ask your government to listen to you? Tell them to send in troops. They could take over the New Orleans port.

* Join some settlers who want to leave the Union? You can form a new nation. Maybe a deal to use the port can be worked out.

MANY STAY IN AMERICA

A small number of Americans moved into Spanish territory. However, most stayed where they were. They were proud to be Americans and were not about to give that up. They remained loyal to the United States.

American troops also never invaded New Orleans. The nation's leaders in Washington, D.C., had other matters on their mind. They were not willing to go to war because some settlers had trouble shipping their goods.

Still, the Spanish did not rest easy. Now they had another fear. This time they were worried about France.

There had been a **revolution**, or uprising, in France. The French king and queen were killed. A new government had taken over. It was to be a **democracy**, or government of the people.

Then in 1799, a strong leader named Napoleon came to power. Napoleon had taken part in the revolution. Yet he

During the French Revolution, people stormed a building called the Bastille on July 14, 1789. Ten years later, Napoleon became France's leader.

ruled as if he were king. He was a man who loved power. Many thought he was **ruthless**.

Napoleon hoped to take over other countries and make them part of France. He had already taken over much of Europe. Now he had his eye on Spain's land in America.

Napoleon spoke to King Charles IV and Queen Maria Luisa of Spain about the territory. He asked for a land trade. He promised them a good deal.

Queen Maria Luisa thought that the whole Louisiana Territory was a big swamp. Actually, only a small part of it was swampy.

Napoleon would get the Louisiana Territory. In return, Spain would get some land in northern Italy. Napoleon had won this area in battle. He called it the Kingdom of Etruria.

The Spanish queen liked the idea. She thought the land in America was just a big swamp. She hoped to have her daughter rule the area in Italy instead.

Napoleon wanted the deal written up as a treaty. But he insisted that it be kept secret. He did not want other countries to know his plans.

Francisco de Goya painted this likeness of Queen Maria Luisa of Spain in 1799.

Napoleon on the Battlefield is a painting that shows the French leader at war.

WHAT WOULD YOU DO?

What if you were the king or queen of Spain?

Would you . . .

✳ **Deal with Napoleon? He has often lied in the past. Would you trust him now?**

HERE'S WHAT HAPPENED:

SPAIN ACCEPTS FRANCE'S DEAL

The Spanish king and queen accepted the deal. They felt that land in Italy would be far more valuable than their territory in America. However, they were disappointed. Napoleon got what he wanted. But no one accepted Spain's rule in northern Italy.

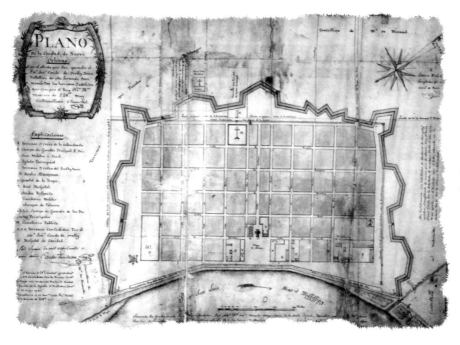

Spaniards made this plan for the city of New Orleans. It was made in 1801, the same year that Spain made a deal to sell the Louisiana Territory to France.

Then in 1801, Thomas Jefferson became president of the United States. He had heard about the secret treaty between France and Spain. This greatly upset him.

Jefferson did not want Napoleon to own land near the United States. He knew that the French leader wanted power. Before long, he would want more land. This could hurt America's growth.

Napoleon (above) wanted to expand his empire. Thomas Jefferson was afraid he would try to do this in the United States.

WHAT WOULD YOU DO?

If you were Jefferson, *would you . . .*

Thomas Jefferson

✳ Act right away? Napoleon has already taken over countries in Europe. Go to war to stop him from taking any land here.

✳ Stay calm? Maybe you can deal with this peacefully. Send someone to France to try to work things out.

ROBERT LIVINGSTON GOES TO FRANCE

Jefferson hoped that things could be settled peacefully. A war would be costly. Lives would be lost as well.

Instead, Jefferson sent his friend Robert Livingston to France. Livingston was to talk to Napoleon as well as others. He had to learn all he could.

This would not be easy. Livingston spoke little French. He also did not hear very well. Yet he was determined to do his best.

Jefferson picked Robert Livingston (above) to go to France.

Was there really a secret treaty? If so, Livingston had to act. He had to make Napoleon not want to come to America.

Napoleon had many enemies in Europe. He did not need the United States as another one. Jefferson was counting on this.

Yet Livingston had a hard time in France. Napoleon was very tricky.

He would not give him any straight answers.

No one else was very helpful either. Others in the government lied. They told Livingston that there was no treaty.

But, Napoleon had an older brother, Joseph. Napoleon would listen to his brother sometimes. Maybe Joseph could help the Americans.

Robert Livingston had been part of the group that wrote the Declaration of Independence. From left to right are Thomas Jefferson, Roger Sherman, Benjamin Franklin, Livingston, and John Adams.

It was likely that Napoleon would send more settlers and troops to North America. Once there, he would want to add to his land.

WHAT WOULD YOU DO?

What if you were Livingston?

Would you . . .

✳ **Try to speak to Joseph?**

✳ **Just go home and tell Jefferson to prepare for war with France?**

LIVINGSTON HAS LITTLE SUCCESS

Livingston did get close to Napoleon's brother. He was of no help, though. Napoleon was known to be stubborn. He rarely changed his mind.

Soon the truth came out anyway. Napoleon no longer felt he had to hide his plans. He hoped to act in April 1802. Five to seven thousand soldiers would be sent to the Louisiana Territory.

Word of this spread. Many Americans in the West were upset. They feared that the port at New Orleans might close for good.

Some called for war. Others were ready to leave the United States. They wanted to make a deal with whoever had the port.

Napoleon planned to send soldiers to the Louisiana Territory.

Fort Condé was France's main fort in the Louisiana Territory. At the left is a replica of the fort in present-day Mobile, Alabama.

WHAT WOULD YOU DO?

If you were Jefferson's advisor, *would you . . .*

* Tell Jefferson to write to Livingston and say that Napoleon should not send troops here? If he does, the United States will side with Great Britain—Napoleon's worst enemy. Napoleon's spies would surely see the letter. They could warn Napoleon not to act.

* Tell Jefferson to have Livingston offer to buy the port of New Orleans? This plan would help both the United States and France. Under it, the United States would allow the French to still use the port. They would not be taxed to do so either.

Here's What Happened:

Jefferson Tries to Make a Deal

Jefferson tried both choices. He wrote the letter to Livingston. He also had Livingston offer to buy New Orleans and the Floridas. The area known as the Floridas still belonged to Spain. However, Jefferson thought the Floridas was owned by France.

Napoleon was not interested in any case. He wanted to enlarge his **empire**.

General Claude Victor-Perrin was to be Napoleon's head military officer in the Louisiana Territory. He would bring the French troops over. The men and supplies that were to go to the Louisiana Territory were waiting for him in Holland.

Jefferson decided to write an important letter to Livingston.

24

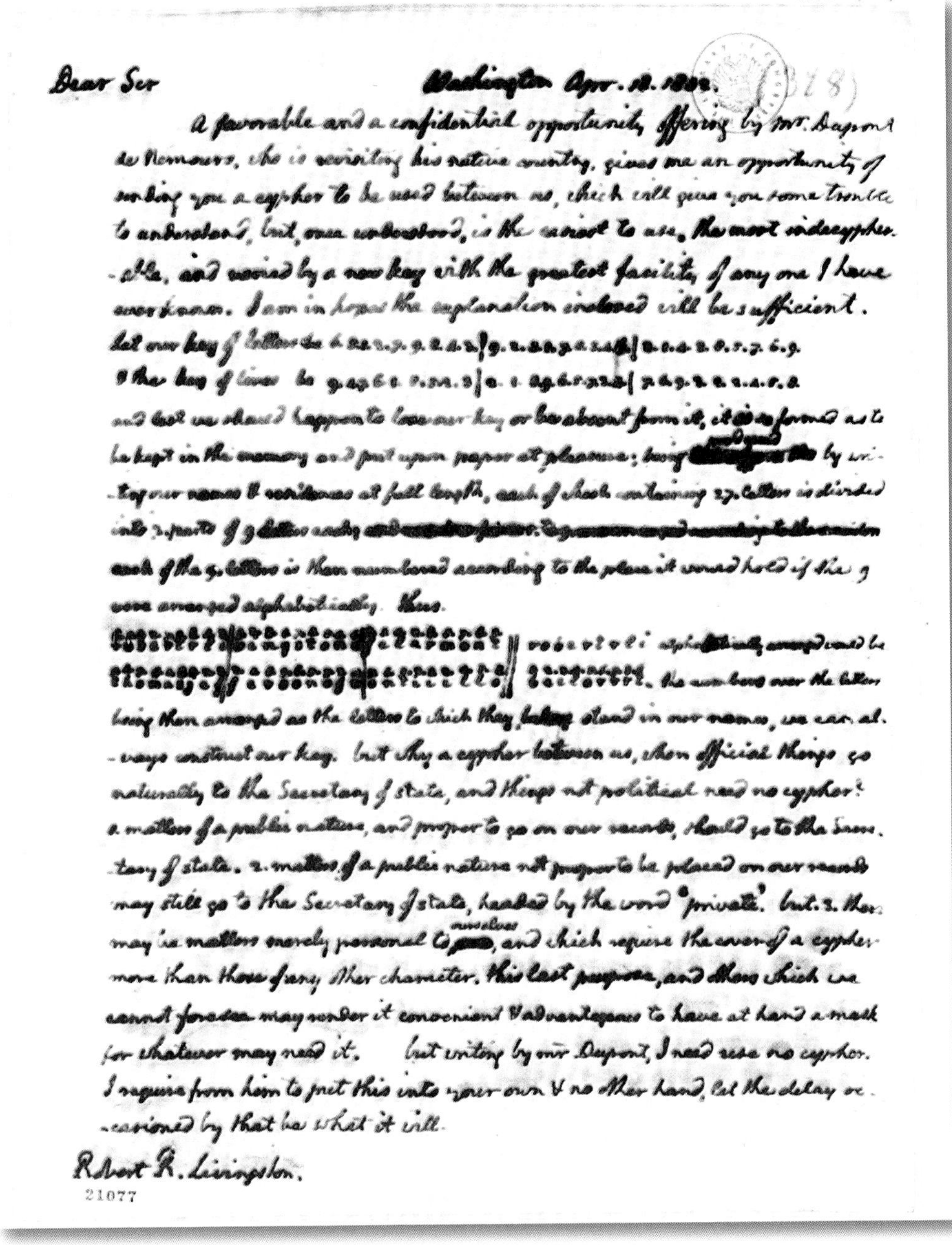

Dear Sir Washington Apr. 18. 1802.

A favorable and a confidential opportunity offering by Mr. Dupont de Nemours, who is revisiting his native country, gives me an opportunity of sending you a cypher to be used between us, which will give you some trouble to understand, but, once understood, is the easiest to use, the most indecypherable, and varied by a new key with the greatest facility of any one I have ever known. I am in hopes the explanation inclosed will be sufficient. let our key of letters be [illegible] & the key of lines be [illegible] and lest we should happen to lose our key or be absent from it, it is so formed as to be kept in the memory and put upon paper at pleasure; being formed by writing our names & residences at full length, each of which containing 27. letters is divided into 3. parts of 9. letters each; [illegible] each of the 9. letters is then numbered according to the place it would hold if the 9 were arranged alphabetically. thus.

[illegible] alphabetically arranged would be [illegible] the numbers over the letters being then arranged as the letters to which they belong stand in our names, we can always construct our key. but why a cypher between us, when official things go naturally to the Secretary of state, and things not political need no cypher? 1. matters of a public nature, and proper to go on our records, should go to the Secretary of state. 2. matters of a public nature not proper to be placed on our records may still go to the Secretary of state, headed by the word "private." but 3. there may be matters merely personal to ourselves, and which require the cover of a cypher more than those of any other character. this last purpose, and others which we cannot foresee may render it convenient & advantageous to have at hand a mask for whatever may need it. but writing by mr Dupont, I need use no cypher. I require from him to put this into your own & no other hand, let the delay occasioned by that be what it will.

Robert R. Livingston.

21077

Above is the first page of a letter that Jefferson wrote to Livingston. In the letter, the president asks Livingston to offer to buy New Orleans and the Floridas.

Yet things did not go as planned. Victor-Perrin was shocked when he got to Holland. Most of the men and supplies were gone.

They had already set sail for another port. They left to bring supplies to the French colony of St. Domingue. Today that colony is the country of Haiti.

Claude Victor-Perrin

In the French colony of St. Domingue, the colonists forced African slaves to work on sugar farms.

WHAT WOULD YOU DO?

Now Napoleon did not have enough men to carry out his plan. What if you were him?

Would you . . .

✳ **Think about Jefferson's offer again? Maybe selling New Orleans would not be so bad after all. Using the port for free would be a plus.**

✳ **Sit tight and wait awhile? Your men and ships will not be gone forever. At this point, you do not have to limit your empire.**

NAPOLEON DOES NOT SELL

Napoleon was not about to sell New Orleans. He had bigger plans for the region.

Until Napoleon's men could take over, the Spanish still ran the port. In October 1802, they changed the port's rules. Americans lost their "right of deposit," meaning they could not leave their goods in New Orleans's **warehouses**.

Flatboats were one of the main ways to move goods up and down the Mississippi River in the early 1800s.

Port of New-Orleans SHUT.

By an Express arrived this evening from New-Orleans, we have received the following important intelligence, which we hasten to give to our readers.—

Extract of a Letter from a gentleman in New-Orleans to his friend in this place, dated Oct. 19, 1802.

"Yesterday the Intendant issued orders, not only for shutting the port of New-Orleans against American vessels coming with cargoes to sell, which was expected; but even totally to prevent the deposit—a step that must produce infinite embarrassment, as well as much loss to many of the citizens of the United States. Two boats that arrived from above yesterday, with flour, were not allowed to land it; consequently cotton, &c coming from Natchez will be in the same predicament."

PROCLAMATION
OF THE
INTENDANT:

AS long as it was necessary to tolerate the trade of neutrals which is now abolished, it would have been prejudicial to this colony, that the Intendant complying with his duty should have prevented the deposit in this city of the property of Americans as granted to them by the 22 article of the Treaty of Friendship, Limits and Navigation of the 27th October, 1795, at the expiration of the three years prefixed; but now that with the publication of the Treaty of Amiens and the re-establishment of the communication between the English and Spanish subjects that inconvenience has ceased, considering that the 22d article of the said treaty prevents my continuing this toleration, which necessity required after the fulfillment of the stipulated time this ministry can no longer consent to it without an express order of the King's. Therefore without prejudice to the exportation of what has been admitted in proper time, I order that from this date shall *cease the privilege which the Americans had of bringing and depositing their goods in this capitol.* And that the foregoing may be publicly known, and that no body may plead ignorance, I order it to be published in the accustomed places, copies to be posted up in public; and that the necessary notice to be given of it to the departments of Finance, Royal Custom-house, and others that may be thought proper. DONE at the Intendancy, signed with my hand, and countersigned by the Notary Public of Finance, at New-Orleans, 16th October, 1802.

(Signed)

JUAN VENTURA MORALES.
By order of the Intendant,
PEDRO PEDESCLAUX.

Herald Office, Natchez, Thursday Night, October 28, 1802.

People learned from newspapers that the port of New Orleans had been closed.

Their goods would not be safely locked away from the time they were taken off the flatboats until they were loaded onto ships. Left out in the open, items could be stolen. Some foods would surely rot.

Napoleon did not have anything to do with this. Yet everyone thought he was behind it. People throughout the United States were angry.

A lot was at stake. Farmers, fur traders, and shop owners were upset. They could lose a great deal of money.

People in both the East and West were hurt by the closing of the port to Americans. People in the East now depended on goods from the West.

Many wanted the government to do something. They wanted to be protected from the whims of foreign nations. They hoped their elected leaders would act.

James Ross was a senator from Pennsylvania. He heard the people's **outcry**. So he brought up a daring idea to Congress.

Ross wanted to send fifty thousand soldiers to New Orleans. They would take over the port. They would fight the French if they had to.

WHAT WOULD YOU DO?

If you were a member of Congress, *would you . . .*

* Vote with Ross and go to war?

* Come up with a more peaceful plan? Have Jefferson raise an army of eighty thousand men. Train them to fight, but try to avoid war. Have the troops ready to go to New Orleans, but do not send them right away.

James Ross wanted to send American soldiers to New Orleans.

CONGRESS AVOIDS WAR

Congress decided against war for now. Yet Jefferson's work was not done. He needed a way to keep the port open.

In January 1803, he sent his friend James Monroe to France. Westerners liked this decision. Monroe owned land in Kentucky. He also wanted the United States to get more land to the West. Westerners felt he would stand up for their rights.

Monroe was to work with Livingston there. Together, they were to get the United States the land its people wanted.

Monroe came at a good time. Things were not going well for Napoleon.

Jefferson sent James Monroe (left) to France to help Livingston.

A French warship had to have room to carry a lot of goods. The sailors also needed places to sleep.

By the winter of 1803, Napoleon had gathered more troops and ships. They were ready to go to America. The winter had been very cold, though. There were large chunks of ice in the sea. The French ships could not sail. This upset Napoleon. The French leader was tired of having his plans delayed.

Many nations feared British ships in the early 1800s. This is a modern reproduction of the *HMS Victory*, a famous British warship.

By March 1803, the ice had melted. Yet now Napoleon faced other problems. The British learned that he was putting together a large fleet.

They did not know that he was going to the United States. The British did not trust Napoleon. They thought he was probably going to attack Great Britain.

The British acted quickly. Their navy formed a **blockade**. Their ships surrounded the ports where the French ships were. Again, the French could not set sail.

WHAT WOULD YOU DO?

What if you were Napoleon?

Would you . . .

✳ **Put off going to New Orleans? The British Navy was much better than the French Navy. In a fight at sea, the French would lose. Many men would die. Ships would be lost as well.**

✳ **Take a chance? The French sailors could try to get past the blockade. Maybe some ships would make it through.**

NAPOLEON DOES NOT ATTACK THE BRITISH

Toussaint L'Ouverture

Napoleon did not want to fight the British at sea. He knew he would not beat England's navy. Napoleon kept his ships in port.

Soon Napoleon got even more bad news. Slaves had **revolted** in St. Domingue. They were led by Toussaint L'Ouverture. And the French soldiers could not put down the revolution. The revolt took a toll on Napoleon's forces. Large numbers of the men died fighting.

By 1791, the African slaves were tired of being beaten and forced to work on the French farms of St. Domingue. They attacked the French.

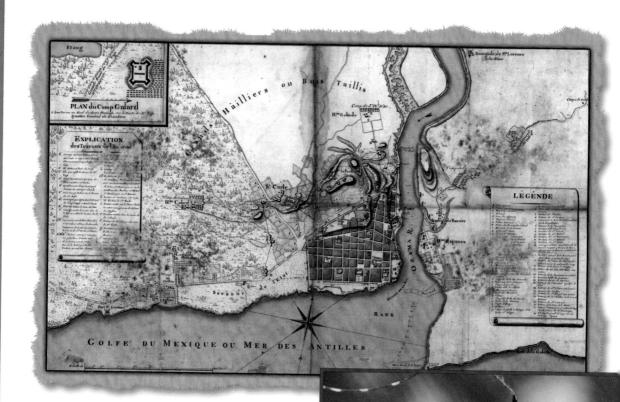

The French camp came up with the plan to attack the slaves in St. Domingue. However, they ran into problems on the island. Many French soldiers died from a disease called yellow fever, which is transmitted through the bite of the Aedes aegypti mosquito shown at the right.

Even more French soldiers died there. These men had gotten **yellow fever**.

St. Domingue had been France's richest colony. Now the colony was gone. The former slaves had made it the nation of Haiti. Napoleon would miss the money that St. Domingue had brought in.

WHAT WOULD YOU DO?

If you were Napoleon, *would you . . .*

* Sell New Orleans to the Americans? This could help France later on. The port and added land would make the United States stronger. In time, the United States could become stronger than Great Britain. Napoleon liked this idea. Great Britain was his worst enemy. He did not want it to be the strongest nation.

* Hold on to your land in America? What if Great Britain took it from the United States? After all, the United States had to fight for its independence from Great Britain. Great Britain might like to have land in America again. This would make it richer and stronger. Britain would be even more able to harm France.

NAPOLEON DECIDES TO SELL

In April 1803, Napoleon had a change of heart. He decided to sell his land in America. However, he wanted to sell more than New Orleans. He hoped the United States would buy all the land in the Louisiana Territory.

Livingston and Monroe had to act quickly. Napoleon wanted the money right away. Within days, he might be at war with Great Britain.

What if you were Livingston or Monroe? You were never told to buy more than New Orleans and the Floridas. You do not have time to ask Jefferson. It would take weeks to send a letter by ship to America. Then you would have to wait several more weeks for an answer.

Monroe (above) and Livingston had a tough decision to make.

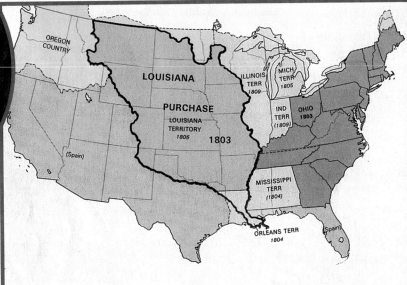

Jefferson (above) was far away in the United States. Monroe and Livingston could only contact him by letter, which took weeks.

See how much bigger the United States is with the Louisiana Territory? Would you buy it?

WHAT WOULD YOU DO?

Would you . . .

* Insist on just buying New Orleans? Perhaps you feel that you cannot buy the rest on your own. Napoleon may refuse, but you cannot help that.

* Act boldly and buy it all? More land will help your nation grow. You think that is what Jefferson would want.

LIVINGSTON AND MONROE MAKE THE LOUISIANA PURCHASE!

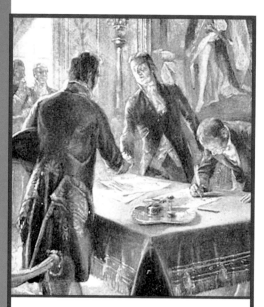

Marquis Francois de Barbe-Marbois of France (left), Robert Livingston (center), and James Monroe sign the Louisiana Purchase Treaty.

Livingston and Monroe took a chance. They agreed to buy all the land. They got it for just $15 million.

Jefferson was thrilled with the new territory. The deal was drawn up as a treaty with France. Congress approved it on October 20, 1803.

It proved to be a good purchase for the United States. It now had the area's ports and rivers. There was plenty of fruitful farmland too. Coal, oil, and iron would be found there

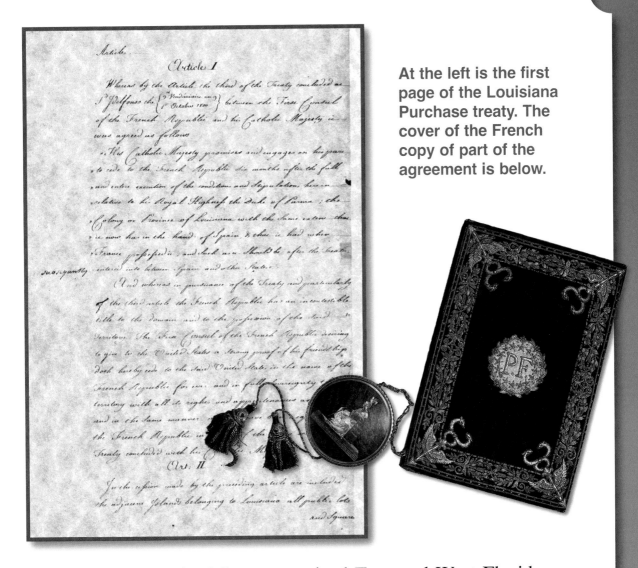

At the left is the first page of the Louisiana Purchase treaty. The cover of the French copy of part of the agreement is below.

as well. The United States acquired East and West Florida from Spain in 1819.

The added area from the Louisiana Purchase made a big difference. It nearly doubled the United States in size. The Louisiana Purchase included all of the present-day states of Arkansas, Missouri, Iowa, Oklahoma, Kansas, and Nebraska. It also included parts of Louisiana, Minnesota, North Dakota, South Dakota, Texas, New Mexico, Wyoming, Montana, and Colorado.

The purchase became famous too. Today it is known as the greatest land deal in American history.

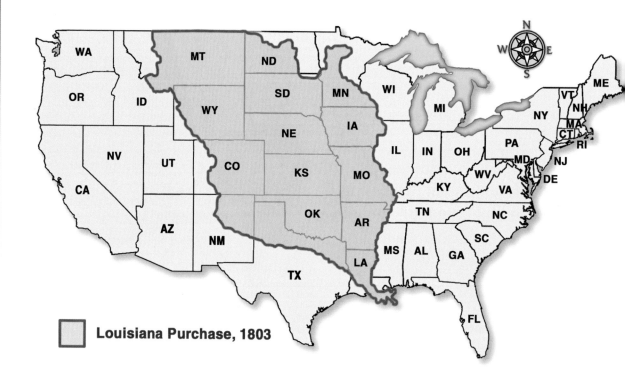

Louisiana Purchase, 1803

This map shows the parts of the present-day states the Louisiana Purchase covered.

TIMELINE

1762—King Louis XV of France gives his cousin King Charles III of Spain the area known as the Louisiana Territory.

1795—The Treaty of San Lorenzo or Pinckney's Treaty is signed between the United States and Spain.

1799—The French leader Napoleon comes to power; he makes a secret deal with Spain to take over the Louisiana Territory.

1800—The United States only reaches as far west as the Mississippi River.

1801—Thomas Jefferson becomes president of the United States; sends Robert Livingston to France.

1802—*April:* Americans learn that Napoleon plans to send thousands of soldiers to the Louisiana Territory; Napoleon's men are delayed and Spain continues to run the port for France.

October: Spain changes the rules for the Port of New Orleans; Americans can no longer leave their goods in warehouses there.

1803—*January:* Thomas Jefferson sends James Monroe to France to try to buy part of the Louisiana Territory.

March: A British blockade stops Napoleon's soldiers from leaving France.

April: Napoleon decides to sell all of the Louisiana Territory to the United States.

October 20: Congress approves the treaty allowing the Louisiana Purchase.

WORDS TO KNOW

blockade—To block off a port by surrounding it with ships.

colonist—A person who settles in a new land.

democracy—A type of government in which people choose their own leaders in elections.

empire—A group of territories with the same ruler.

flatboat—A boat with a flat bottom used to carry a heavy load of freight along a waterway.

outcry—The act of a lot of people complaining loudly about something.

pelt—An animal skin with fur on it.

pioneer—Someone who settles in new territory.

port—A city where ships can load and unload their cargo.

revolt—To rebel against a government.

revolution—An uprising against a government.

ruthless—Cruel and having no pity.

territory—A large area of land.

treaty—An agreement between nations.

warehouse—A large building used for storing goods.

yellow fever—A tropical disease carried by a mosquito.

LEARN MORE

Books

Burgan, Michael. *The Louisiana Purchase.* Minneapolis, Minn.: Compass Point Books, 2002.

Kozar, Richard. *Lewis and Clark: Explorers of the Louisiana Purchase.* New York: Chelsea House, 2000.

Raabe, Emily. *Thomas Jefferson and the Louisiana Purchase.* New York: Powerkids Press, 2003.

Ribke, Simone T. *Thomas Jefferson.* Danbury, Conn.: Children's Press, 2003.

Roop, Peter and Connie Roop. *The Louisiana Purchase.* Milestone Books, 2004.

Internet Addresses

The Louisiana Purchase Exhibit
<http://www.loc.gov/rr/program/bib/ourdocs/louisiana.htm>
Visit this great Web site for lots of information on that very famous land deal. Be sure to check out the historical maps.

Monticello: The Home of Thomas Jefferson
<http://www.monticello.org/jefferson/lewisandclark/louisiana.html>
Visit the famous home of Thomas Jefferson where he spent hours deciding the best strategy for the Louisiana Purchase.

The Port of New Orleans
<http://www.portno.com/>
Back in Jefferson's day, everyone wanted the port of New Orleans. It is still an important seaport today. Visit its Web site and learn all about it.

INDEX